The Original
Peter Rabbit ™
Baby Book

My First Year

Frederick Warne

FREDERICK WARNE

Published by the Penguin Group
Penguin Books Ltd, 80 Strand, London WC2R 0RL, England
Penguin Putnam Inc., 375 Hudson Street, New York 10014, USA
Penguin Books Australia Ltd, 250 Camberwell Road, Camberwell, Victoria 3124, Australia
Penguin Books Canada Ltd, 10 Alcorn Avenue, Toronto, Ontario, Canada M4V 3B2
Penguin Books India (P) Ltd, 11 Community Centre, Panchsheel Park, New Delhi 110 017, India
Penguin Group (NZ), 67 Apollo Drive, Rosedale, North Shore 0632, New Zealand
Penguin Books (South Africa) (Pty) Ltd, P O Box 9, Parklands 2121, South Africa

Penguin Books Ltd, Registered Offices: 80 Strand, London WC2R 0RL, England

Web site at: www.peterrabbit.com

This new edition first published by Frederick Warne 2005
23
Original concept and title devised by Judy Taylor for first edition 1983

This edition copyright © Frederick Warne & Co., 2005
New reproductions of Beatrix Potter's book illustrations copyright © Frederick Warne & Co., 2002
Original text and illustrations copyright © Frederick Warne & Co.,
1902, 1904, 1905, 1906, 1907, 1908, 1909, 1910, 1917, 1918, 1922, 1930
Frederick Warne & Co. is the owner of all rights, copyrights and trademarks
in the Beatrix Potter character names and illustrations.

ISBN: 9780723256830

Printed and bound in China

THE KEEPSAKE POCKET

In the back of this book, there is a pocket where you
can store precious mementos. The first few months after
your baby's arrival are busy ones and you may not always have
time to update this journal as regularly as you would like.
Instead, you may find it easier to make rough notes in your
spare time, and store them in the keepsake pocket, along with
your prenatal scans, and favourite photographs (remember to
write the date and a brief comment on the back). You may also
like to keep a lock of your baby's hair, your baby's hospital
bracelet, or other special items in the keepsake pocket.

About My Parents

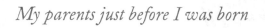

My parents just before I was born

My father's name
Steve Boyer

My mother's name
Kirby Boyer

Waiting for Me

My prenatal scans

Ideas for Names

Boys' names

Mercer

Girls' names

Eloise June

My parents' feelings about my arrival

A was very different than Madeline. You came very quickly and we were so glad you did! We were so excited to meet you

My Arrival

My name is

Eloise June Boyer

I was born on

9/3/15

at

5:14 pm

I weighed

7 lbs 2 oz

I measured (length)

19 1/2"

My eyes were

Blue

My hair was

Blonde

My first picture

My Birth Story

Where I was born
Anne Arundel Med Center

Midwife's name

Doctor's name

Birth partner's name
Daddy

My birth

My parents' feelings when I arrived

My First Few Days

Soon after I arrived home

Emme & Poppy

Pappy

My visitors
Aunt Morgan & Uncle Brendan
Charlotte Betsy Walker
Alex & Gavin & Annie
Aunt 'tine & Madison
Uncle Mark Murphy
Mom Mom

Settling In

I came home on

9/5/15

My First Night

I fell asleep at

8 pm

I woke up at

11 pm

I fell asleep at

12:00

I woke up again at

2:30 am

I fell asleep at

3:00

I woke up yet again at

6:00 am

My sleeping patterns in my first week

Improved! You gave mommy sleep! ☺ mommy napped with you everyday!

My feeding patterns in my first week

every 3-4 hours

My parents' first impressions

We just were *So* in love with our two girls ♡ ♡ ♡

My Hands and Feet

My hand and footprints at two weeks

Gifts, Cards and Flowers

A Record

_____

_____

_____

_____

_____

_____

_____

_____

_____

_____

_____

_____

_____

_____

_____

_____

_____

_____

About My Name

Photograph of me at (age)

_____

My name means   My name was chosen by

_____   _____

The reason why my name was chosen

_____

_____

_____

My Family Tree

Great Grandparents	Great Grandparents	Great Grandparents	Great Grandparents
Mom Mom		Grandma Dar	

Grandfather	Grandmother	Grandfather	Grandmother
Pappy Boyer	Cindy West Boyer	Poppy	Emme

Aunts/Uncles	~~Mother~~ Father	~~Father~~ Mother	Aunts/Uncles
Ryan/Abby Jacob Hannah Maggie	Steve Boyer	Kirby Boyer	Morgan/Brendan

Brothers	Me	Sisters
	Eloise	Madeline

Moving Around

Use this page to record special moments as your baby grows more independent

	DATE	AGE
I lifted my head		
I rolled over		
I sat alone		
I moved around or crawled		
I pulled myself up		
I took my first steps		

Photograph of me sitting alone

Talking

*Use this page to record special moments as
your baby communicates with you*

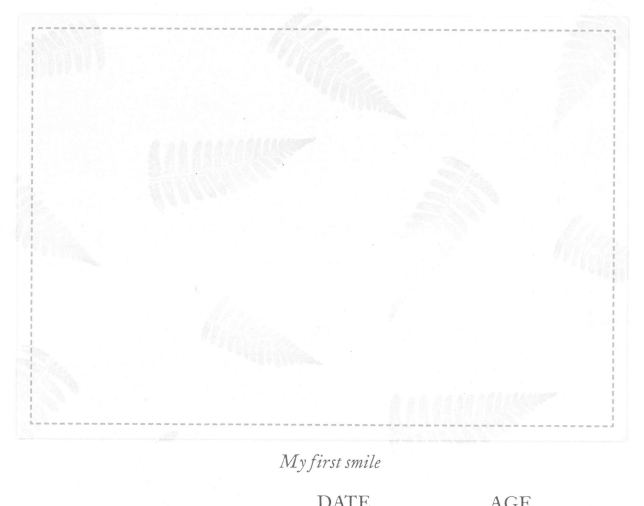

My first smile

	DATE	AGE
I smiled		
I laughed		
I babbled`		
I copied noises		
I started 'singing'		

Family and Friends

*Use these pages to record special moments as your baby
gets to know friends and family*

I moved my eyes to watch you (date)

_____

at (weeks/months)

_____

Comments

_____

_____

_____

_____

I smiled for special people (date)   at (weeks/months)

_____   _____

Comments

_____   _____

I said your name (date)   at (weeks/months)

_____   _____

Comments

_____   _____

A photograph of me with

_____

I cuddled you (date)   at (weeks/months)

_____   _____

Comments

_____

_____

_____

First Experiences

*Use these pages to describe unforgettable outings
as your baby begins to explore the world*

I first went swimming (date)   at (weeks/months)

Comments

I first went to the playground (date)   at (weeks/months)

9/9/15   6 days old

Comments

You and mommy had the best
time watching Daddy & Madelin
play!

I went to my first party (date)

at (weeks/months)

Comments

I went on my first holiday (date)

_____

at (weeks/months)

_____

Comments

_____

_____

_____

_____

I wore my first pair of shoes (date)   at (weeks/months)

_____   _____

Comments

_____

_____

I had my first haircut (date)   at (weeks/months)

_____   _____

Comments

_____

_____

Special Occasions

Use these pages to mark religious festivals, special naming ceremonies or celebrations in the first year

Mealtimes

I tried my first solids (date)

_____

at (weeks/months)

_____

Comments

_____

_____

_____

_____

I tried puréed food (date)   at (weeks/months)

_____   _____

Comments

_____

_____

	DATE	AGE
I tried finger food		
I tried chopped food		
I first held a spoon		
I fed myself		
I drank from a beaker		

My favourite foods

_____

_____

_____

_____

_____

My least favourite foods

_____

_____

_____

_____

_____

A photograph of me in my high chair

Bathtime

Me in the baby bath

My favourite bath toys

_____

_____

_____

_____

_____

_____

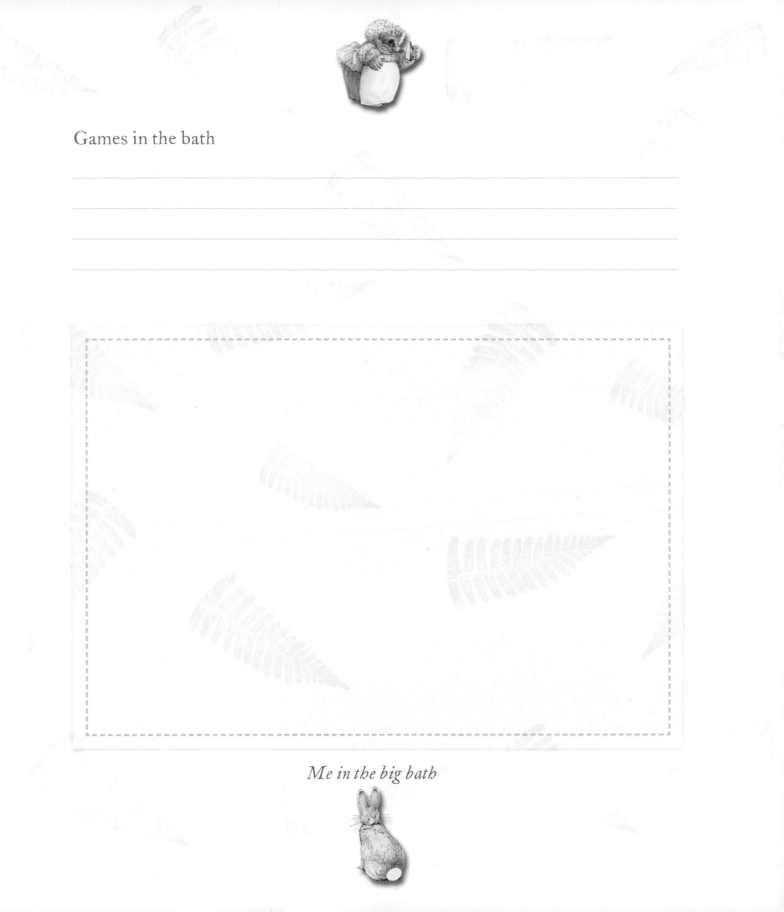

Games in the bath

_____

_____

_____

_____

Me in the big bath

Bedtime

Bedtimes change as babies grow up. Use these pages to help you record bedtimes in the first year

My bedtime is at

_____

Date (weeks/months)

_____

Evening routines in the first year

_____

_____

_____

_____

I moved to a cot (date)   at (weeks/months)

_____   _____

Comments

_____

_____

I slept through the night (date)   at (weeks/months)

_____   _____

Comments

_____

_____

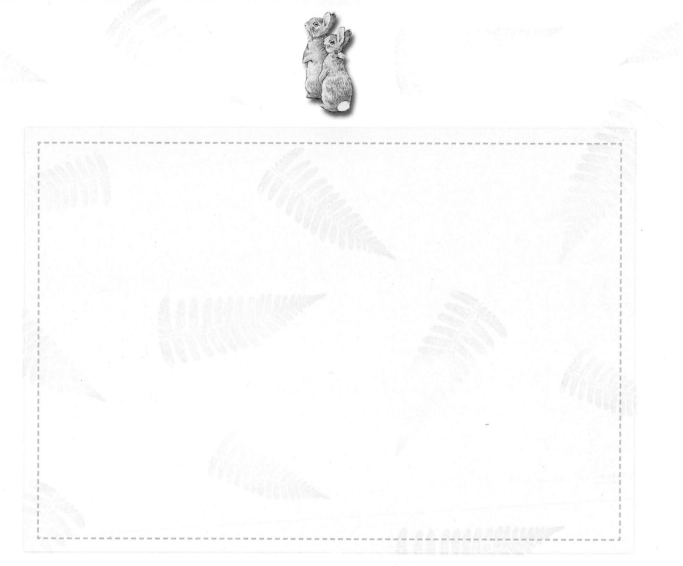

Me in my pyjamas

My favourite books, toys and lullabies at bedtime

_____

_____

_____

_____

_____

Playing Games

*Use these pages to help you record
what made your baby laugh*

First games

_____

_____

_____

_____

Things that make me laugh

_____

_____

_____

_____

People that make me laugh

_____

_____

_____

_____

_____

_____

_____

Me with one of my favourite toys

My favourite songs

_____
_____
_____
_____
_____

My favourite toys

_____
_____
_____
_____

My Health

Immunisations	DATE	AGE
Eyesight tests		
Hearing tests		
Childhood illnesses		
Allergies		
Blood group		
Doctor		

My Teeth

The first tooth can appear at any time in the first or second year.
When the first tooth appears, write in the date next to number 1
on the list below. Then number the relevant tooth in the diagram, and so on.

DATE

1 _____

2 _____

3 _____

4 _____

5 _____

6 _____

7 _____

8 _____

9 _____

10 _____

Upper

Right

Left

Lower

DATE

11 _____

12 _____

13 _____

14 _____

15 _____

16 _____

17 _____

18 _____

19 _____

20 _____

Some babies find teething a struggle,
some hardly notice. This is how
I behaved while I was teething.

_____

_____

_____

_____

My Baby Record

THREE MONTHS

Me at three months

Weight   Length

_____   _____

Comments

_____

_____

_____

_____

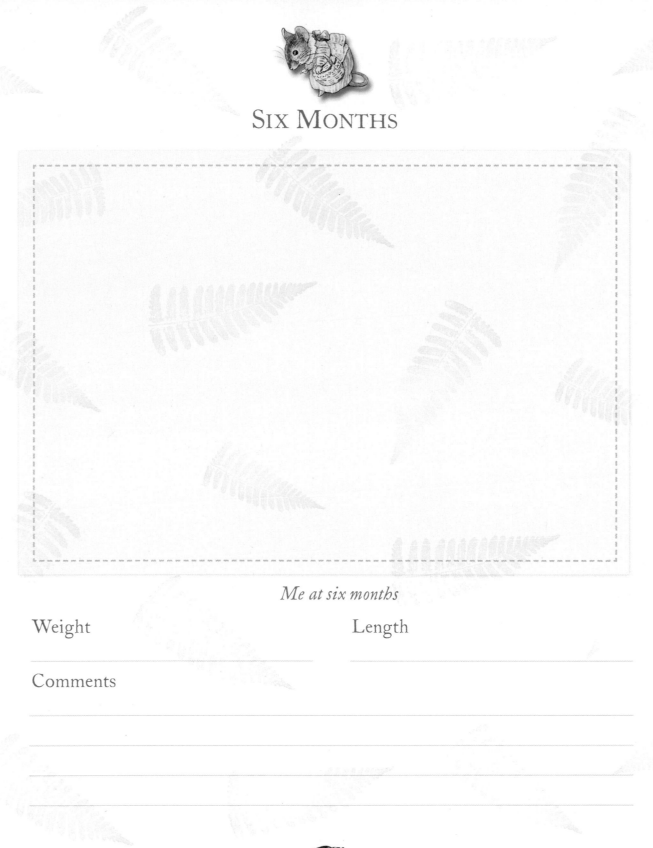

SIX MONTHS

Me at six months

Weight

Length

Comments

My Baby Record

NINE MONTHS

Me at nine months

Weight   Length

Comments

Twelve Months

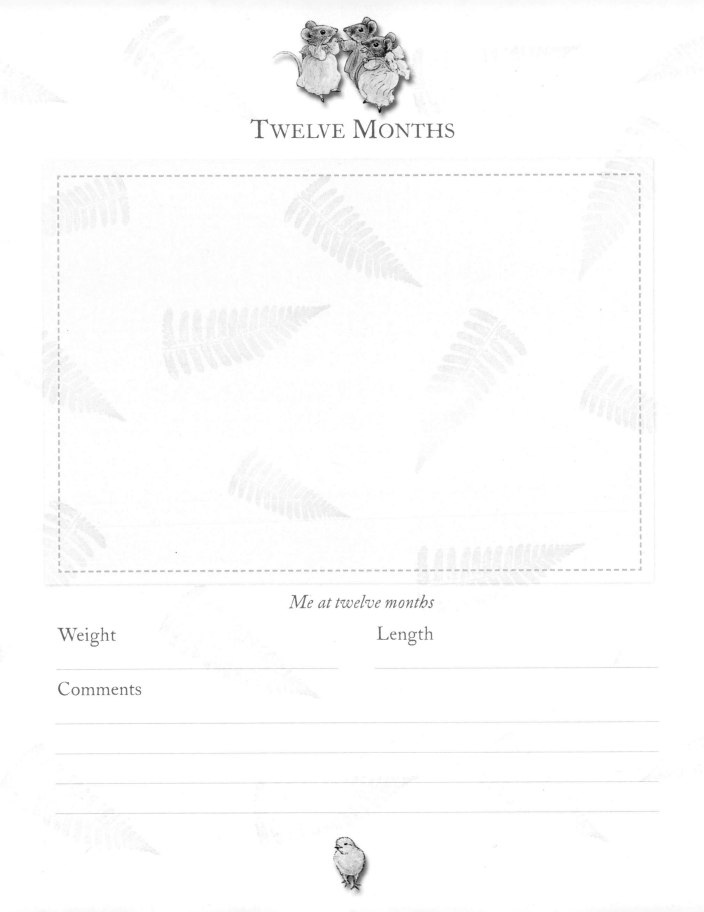

Me at twelve months

Weight _____   Length _____

Comments

_____

_____

_____

_____

My Hands and Feet

My hand and footprints at one year

Artistic Talents

My first scribble

My First Birthday

Me on my first birthday

Description of the day

_____

_____

_____

_____

Presents

_____
_____
_____
_____
_____
_____
_____
_____

Who visited

_____
_____
_____
_____

My birthday cake (*who bought or made it, and what it looked like*)

_____
_____
_____
_____

The End of My First Year

Comments *(my parents' feelings, and a summary of the last twelve months)*

_____

_____

_____

_____

_____

_____